SHOWMEN'S ENGINES AT WAR

By Kay Townsend

Never before has there been so much information gathered on this subject.

Kay58@fsmail.net

K Townsend

Front cover photo work
by
BarkerARTLINE@aol.com

Cover photo
Fowler 14868, *The Princess*
Taken in Little Britain
London, 1941.

Published in 2009

Email: kay58@fsmail.net

ISBN 978-0-9553595-2-1

Also written by Kay Townsend:

Townsends – A Showman's Story
The Showman's Forgotten Scammells

Cover design and print by Creeds Telephone: **01308 423411** Web: **www.creedsuk.com**

ACKNOWLEDGMENTS

Thank you to the people below,
My husband, David Castleman and especially
Ron Dawe of the Road Locomotive Society,
Les Burberry – photos from the Road Locomotive Society,
The late Alan Duke – notes from The Road Loco Society,
Allan Downs – photo collection,
Bill Brian – photo collection,
Shane Seagrave – proof reading.

Bibliography

The Burrell book by Michael Lane published 1971.

For help and information

Peter Parrish, Stephen Bailey, Philip Upchurch
and Barnaby Newton. Also, thank you to the numerous people
I spoke to and who contributed information.

Without their help this book would not have been possible.

INDEX

SHOWMEN'S ENGINES AT WAR

How this book came to be

When writing a book about the fairgrounds during WWII I found, whilst gathering information on the showmen's engines doing work of national importance, that a large amount of information was coming my way. Because I had more literature than I required, I did consider discarding some of this information, but then realised, never in one place has there been so much information gathered on the showmen's engines working in war time.

I decided this must not be discarded but must go to print, so I have produced this small book on a subject which needed to be congealed into one publication. I have asked Showmen to come forward with their stories, however, with most of the elder generation gone, some show names have escaped me.

Engines that departed from showland **before** the war years, (so were no longer owned by a showman) are not included, as this publication is of the showmen's engines leaving or working with a family to help this nation in its hour of need.

1939

By 1939, Industry was ahead of the showmen, in phasing out the traction engine in favour of the lorry. By the war years the showmen were in the midst of this change-over themselves, with only about 80 engines remaining in service on the fair grounds.

When war was declared, September 3rd 1939, most showmen closed down, some did manage to open weeks later, some at Christmas but most not until spring 1940. At first we had the "phoney war" where very little happened in the way of enemy attacks, then the first bomb to land on London was August 24th 1940.

Attacks became more frequent and on September 7th the Luftwaffe switched from airfield attacks to the City of London, which became known as the "blitz." With the inner cities being densely built upon, the damaged and unsafe shells of buildings after these raids was a problem and this had to be dealt with. This is where the showmen's engines were needed.

When war commenced the Government knew what to expect to some degree and knew civilian transport would be needed. In WWI the Showmen's transport of time was the horse and traction engine, and the Government exercised their power by requisition. After the war some engines were returned to the showmen, some were not.

Horses were also taken and, in some cases, they had been put through so much that, when returned, they were knackered and destroying them would have been the kindest thing to do. Now, in this second war, things would be different.

WWI.

This is *Empress of the South* Burrell no 2562, which belonged to my grandfather, Richard Townsend, of Weymouth. The engine was taken to work at Wilton, in Wiltshire and was returned when the work was finished.

This book will concentrate mainly on the engines of WWII, with information from the sons who were youngsters at the time but can just remember their engines and, in some cases, at the age of eleven had driven the engine.

When researching this book I found, in many cases, that the families believed their father's engines were requisitioned as they were in the First World War. In some cases it seems possible, however, with the elder generation now gone, to prove this is difficult.

The Government had the powers to requisition vehicles and may have, in a few cases. However, you will now read how the Showmen's Guild were approached and held information on the **hiring** of vehicles.

Because Britain had been preparing for war for some time, soon after the declaration the Showmen's Guild was approached by the Government and asked to put a call out for members to come forward for future work.

Because the traction engine was loosing its popularity, the showmen put little value to the now outdated machines and, in some cases, were only too happy for them to do essential work and, by doing so, felt they were helping their country.

The first Showmen's Guild meeting after the hostilities commenced was held at the *World's Fair* offices at Oldham on September 19th 1939. This emergency meeting had thirteen items on the agenda.

Item ten was:

"That Central Office furnishes any information which comes to hand regarding work of national importance, which was likely to be beneficial to the members."

This included labour and the use of the showmen's transport by the

Ministry of Transport,
Roads & Bridges,
Ministry of Supply,
Timber Haulage.

So what was the demand for transport?

The Government were so desperate for all forms of transport that they widened the scope of the 'C' licence, which restricted showmen to carrying their own goods, and made them equal to the 'A' licence, to carry anything anywhere.

Many showmen took advantage of this and went into road haulage. Here are two advertisements which were placed in the showmen's weekly newspaper "The World's Fair":

WANTED FOR HIRE

RELIABLE LORRIES and TRAILERS required.
For long jobs commencing early November.
For full details
THE TRANSPORT OFFICE,
142 BATH ROAD, HOUNSLOW.

SURPLUS PLANT and MACHINERY required
to satisfying urgent requirements.
Especially diesel engines, diesel generating sets,
A.C motors, D.C motors, needed for work of
National Importance.
GEORGE COHEN & SONS CO LTD,
Wood Lane, London and Stanningley, nr Leeds.

So despite the Government's power to requisition, it was a matter of choice if the showmen wanted their transport to take part in war duties.

Soon the Forestry Commission, based in Bristol, also contacted the Showmen's Guild, requiring much needed transport for timber clearing and haulage.

At the same time the Showmen's Guild placed this announcement in the *World's Fair* paper:

> **ENGINES FOR HAULAGE WORK**
>
> *The Guild central office has data available as to the working costs for the hiring of traction engines or lorries for haulage work. Any member, who is likely to take on work of this description, should contact the Guild General Secretary for more information.*

Retired showman Kevin Collins, whose father had engines working on demolition in Manchester, believes his father was paid on a daily rate. Some showmen worked independently with their own engine; others hired themselves and engine over to the Authorities or a contractor.

Now you will see what those engines **not** on the fairground were doing. Also, do bear in mind, when reading a story about a family working with their engine, that **some** families also remained open with their fair and would only do essential work in the winter months, whilst others did both at the same time.

WE ARE PRIVILEGED TO SEE PHOTOS

Occasionally you will come across photos taken by the late Philip Bradley. During the war years there were restrictions on photography, with one set of rules for the press and different rules for the amateur/ enthusiast. Bradley, being an enthusiast, had to be very careful. The following was written by Bradley on what it was like for him to obtain some of the photos we are privileged to see in this book:

"*Cameras were easily available but a 35mm film was for the wealthy, ordinary mortals paid a shilling for an 8-frame roll. Wartime photography brought problems, as one or two enthusiasts were silly enough to try and conceal their cameras about their person immediately after use! The Ministry of Home Security had produced an explicit, and not unduly restrictive, schedule of rules defining the subjects barred to amateur photographers. Subjects forbidden were damage by enemy action. So, when visiting fairs in the war years, I had a copy of the Ministry regulations in my pocket and I carried my camera quite openly.*"

Philip Bradley (1920-99) lived in Ewell, Surrey and bequeathed his unique photo collection to The Surrey History Centre, Woking. Here you can view his archive, by appointment, and also request copies of his photos.

Every effort has been made to secure the relevant permission to reproduce the images contained in this book. Any errors or omissions are unintentional and details should be forwarded to the author.

THRESHING

THE PHILADELPHIA

Burrell 3413, reg CR 5826* The Philadelphia *at Bishops Waltham, May 1932. *Copyright unknown.*

On the 16th of Sept 1912, Charles Burrell & Sons of Thetford, delivered a 6 n.h.p. engine no 3413 to Wareham Station (Dorset) for showman Joseph Smith of Southampton. He named the engine *The Philadelphia* and the name is still on the engine today.

When Joseph Smith died, the engine passed to his widow and son, William, who in the mid-30s hired it and then eventually sold it to showman Alf Bartlett of Fordingbridge, Hampshire. Alf not only bought *The Philadelphia* but also the Smith Gallopers as well; so on the fairgrounds *The Philadelphia* continued the job of working with the Gallopers.

Alexander Park, Portsmouth 1939.
By George Tucker. National Fairground Archive, Sheffield.

At the outbreak of the war in 1939 Alf Bartlett decided not to travel and so *The Philadelphia* went on to do war work.

After the blockading by enemy shipping, life was difficult trying to feed a nation. Agricultural Contractors were given the run of farms for ploughing/threshing etc, and that is what *The Philadelphia's* work entailed, powering threshing machines for the Ministry of Supply.

One of the farms on which the engine worked was Castle View Farm, Gussage All Saints, near Wimborne, Dorset, with farm contractor William Everett & Sons. The dynamo was removed by Alf Bartlett before he parted with the engine and the canopy was cut back, whilst on the farm, to make it more manoeuverable. The dynamo platform and some fittings were also removed but, thankfully, all parts were kept.

When the work was finished, *The Philadelphia* was parked opposite the farm until 1958, and then was moved under cover into a Nissen hut.

Still outside, taken in 1958.
By the late Archie Parrish.

So this engine never returned to Alf Bartlett, but stood for 48 years waiting for preservation.

In 1966 John Newton of Hungerford saw the engine and, on several occasions over the years, he tried to purchase it.

In February 1999, 33 years after first wanting to buy *The Philadelphia,* John and his wife Brenda acquired the engine.

News then travelled around the world that it had survived, which caused quite a stir in the steam world. It took six years of restoration, and in 2007 *The Philadelphia* was entered into preservation by John and can now be seen on the rally fields.

Photo by Stephen Bailey.

Thank you to Mr John Newton and Stephen Bailey for supplying this information.

ARTHUR BATES

A National news paper reported on October 18th 1942:

> SHOWMEN HELP TO THRESH HARVEST
>
> Mr Arthur Bates has had his gilded traction engine stood in some south Lancashire farmyard with its belts driving a thrashing machine, where for years it has been driving the Dodgems. Months ago the Minister of Agriculture suggested the showmen could help with the forthcoming harvest.

HELPING IN THE HARVEST

Bottom left, Mr Bates, with Miss Jennings and Miss Agnes Bell also helping.

This showman's name came up twice for doing war work. Arthur Bates had three engines in his ownership. The name of his engine above was not mentioned in the newspaper article.

However by looking at the dates he parted with his engines and going by the width of the rear wheel on the engine, it is almost certain to be his 7 n.h.p. Burrell 3817 *Perseverance.*

***Burrell 3817* Perseverance.**
Photo by B.D. Stoyel.

The Bates family took delivery of this one in 1919. The threshing photo was taken in 1943, the very same year he advertised the engine for sale, so it was not threshing for long

This was not one of the best looking showmen's engines as it had twisted brass canopy supports but no other brass fittings. Nevertheless, the engine was always clean and well polished by the owner.

Working with the Bates Ark ride, being just one of their machines from 1932 until 1950s.
From National Fairground Archives, Sheffield.

The only other engine in his ownership at the time was Foster *Her Majesty,* no 3664, reg TB 2966. But this engine was seen working in Liverpool.

Foster* Her Majesty, *no 3664, reg TB 2966.
Road Loco Society collection.

Her Majesty *seen here working in Liverpool.*
Liverpool Library Archives.

This engine disappeared, so it is thought it was scrapped some time after 1944.

THE DOWNS

London showman Allan Downs was not open when war was declared and, early on in the war, had been on contract work with a road roller. Later, Allan was using his own engine and working for The War Agricultural Committee which entailed threshing around Colchester and the Westbury area.

From the Allan Downs collection.

His engine he used for threshing was a Tiger Tractor, Fowler no 14412, reg U4662 which he also named *Tiger.* This engine has survived and is now in preservation.

THE MAY

From the Allan Downs collection.

The May 4 n.h.p. Burrell no 3453, reg AH 0117 was owned by the show family Sedgwicks and travelled around Lancashire with their Lion show.

This engine ended up doing farm work during the war years then, in 1949, John Downs paid £4 10 shillings for the engine.

He parked it with several other engines on Great Bentley village green and it was due to be cut up along with all the others.

When John was cutting the engines and it came to *The May*, John said *"I want to keep this one."* So *The May* returned to showland with John and travelled with his Gallopers. This engine was fitted with large belly-tanks giving it a range of about 25 miles before re-watering. *The May* is still with the Downs family today.

Information courtesy of Allan Downs.

NICHOLS

Works photo.

Princess Mary is a 8 n.h.p. Burrell 3949, reg no 8287, built in 1923 for William Nichols of Forest Gate, London. When built, one stipulation Mr Nichols had was that the canopy be lower for driving under low bridges. On the fairground it powered his Chair-o-Plane ride.

In 1940, William Nichols put this engine to war work by doing threshing on farms in the Essex area. He was driving the engine himself along with Harry Butlin.

In 1943, after two years on the farms, the family decided to sell the engine. The second owner was showman Charles Presland, so this engine returned to the fairgrounds.

In 1958 *Princess Mary* entered preservation when purchased by Dr T.R Green, then later owned by Commander J.M Baldock of Liphook, Hampshire, then T Lagar to work with the Razzle Dazzle at Penwith Pleasure Beach, Cornwall. In 1983 it was sold to David Hedgeman of Wareham, Dorset.

STARLIGHT: FAIRGROUND TO THRESHING

Road Locomotive Society Archives.

Starlight, Burrell no 3836 was delivered in 1920 and spent the first three years of her life doing timber hauling in Buckinghamshire. Then it had three commercial owners before, in 1934, being purchased by Amusement Caterers Robert Edwards & Sons of Swindon, who eventually converted it to showmen's and used it for his Dodgems.

From the FHT collection.

In 1943, Bob Edwards decided to sell his engines, so all three engines, *Starlight, Earl Kitchener* and *Progress*, were parked in the centre of the yard and contractor Fred Darby of Ely, Cambridgeshire, was to be offered the option of buying all three. However, one of Bob's sons, Albert, did not want to part with all three so Mr Darby asked if he could have just one engine. He was told he could have *Starlight.*

He used the engine to meet the war demand for threshing, which the engine did for the remaining war years. *Starlight* is still with us today and for many years was rallied by former British motorcycle racing champion Dan Shorey of Banbury, Oxfordshire.

BUTTERWORTH

From the Butterworth collection.

John James Butterworth of Rochdale, Lancashire, had engine *Royal Jubilee* Fowler 15121, reg WR 6634. It was built in 1920 for the water works and then passed to the Lancashire County Council. John purchased the engine from the Council in about 1935.

He converted it to a showmen's, to work alongside his Gallopers.

In the summer of 1940, he put the engine on work of National importance by doing threshing around the Manchester area.

When the war ended the Butterworths still retained the engine working on the fairground.

In 1948, John sold it to a Mr Hackney of Cheshire.

Sadly, *Royal Jubilee* is no longer with us. She was last seen in 1952 and must have had a quiet ending, as the engine has never been heard of to this day.

Thank you to Jane Butterworth, for helping with this information.

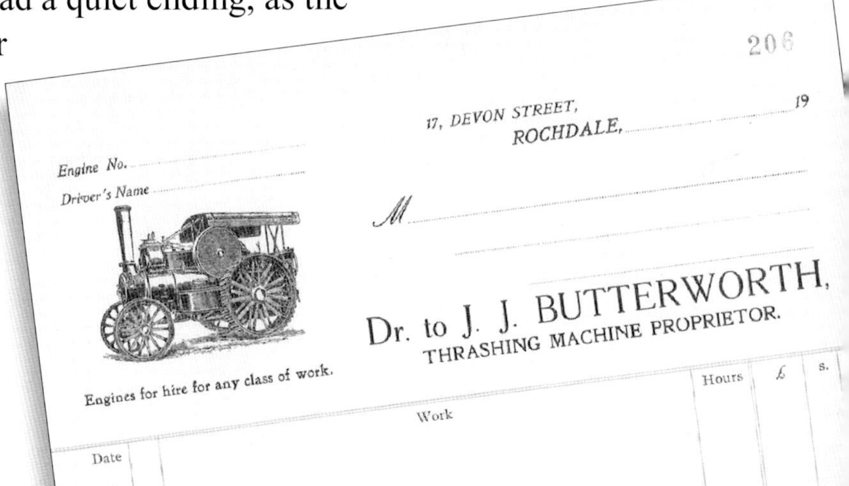
206

17, DEVON STREET,
ROCHDALE, ... 19

Engine No. ....
Driver's Name ....

M ....

Engines for hire for any class of work.

Dr. to J. J. BUTTERWORTH,
THRASHING MACHINE PROPRIETOR.

Date	Work	Hours	£	s.

SILCOCK

Burrell no 3714, reg BN 4885 a 7 n.h.p., was new on April 3rd 1916 and went to circus family H. Shuttleworth of Lancashire, who named it *Violet Lily.*

Rainford 1939. *By R. Scott.*

In 1932, it was then acquired by showman Herbie Silcock of Cheshire, to work with his Ark ride.

In 1940, with machinery needed to help on the farms around the Cheshire and South Lancs area, Herbie first put *Violet Lily* on a farm to work, but this was only for a short time, as he acquired an agricultural engine complete with threshing machine, so then *Violet Lily* returned to work on the fairground. During the harvest season Herbie worked on his threshing machine himself, for contractor Walter Fitter of Warrington. Then Herbie would return to open his fair every night and he did this through to the end of the war in August 1945. *Violet Lily* remained with Herbie until the end of her working days in 1951.

Thank you to Edward Silcock for helping with this information.

AIRFIELDS

ARTHUR HOLLAND

Showman Arthur Holland of Swadlincote, Derbyshire, had two engines helping with the war effort, *Prince Bert* and *Victory*.

Ilkeston 1932. *J. Mellor collection.*

The family were open with their fair at Newark, Nottinghamshire when war was declared. Arthur was allowed to continue opening on the condition they close before dusk. Whilst there, Arthur discovered a local contractor was about to start building an Aerodrome at Swinderby, Lincolnshire. The land consisted of four farms which were commandeered; the families reluctantly moved out at the last minute, leaving fruit on the trees and vegetables in the garden.

Arthur managed to find work there for one of his engines. He used Foster *Prince Bert* 12620, reg AY 9838 which also did work in WWI. His son Bert drove the engine for this work and had to sign on and off for work each day. Arthur also had his lorries doing haulage on the site usually delivering sewer pipes which were so heavy the men rolled them off the lorry. Two pipes would usually be broken doing this but, without the lifting gear, this was the quickest way of doing it.

Meanwhile *Victory* Burrell no 3724, reg AY 9836 was new to Arthur Holland in July, 1916. This engine did not carry twisted brass canopy supports, brass rings or stars. The name was painted on the motion side plates and the flywheel was spoked with a disc cover.

Originally *Victory* worked with the Holland's Scenic Motor Cars, then later used for the Dodgems. In 1940 it was put to work at Forbeck, Lincolnshire, then later it moved to Conningsby to help extend a runway. The contractor also manage to obtain a caterpillar tractor to help with this work, however the caterpillar managed to get stuck and was unable to move. *Victory* was used to pull the Caterpillar out. Through the winter *Victory* did four months work at Conningsby. Later Arthur billed the firm for the work but was never paid, so he had nothing for doing four months work. Eventually, more big American equipment was coming over to help with the war effort, so the engines were no longer needed.

From 1940, "Holiday At Home" fairs were taking place all over the country to boost morale. When Coventry took heavy bombing, "Holiday At Home" fairs were held around the city and *Prince Bert* opened on the Memorial Park Common, powering Arthur's Moonrocket ride. Sadly neither engines are with us any more.

I would like to thank Arthur's son,
Mr Alex Holland for this information.

WILLIAMS OF HAMPSHIRE

In 1939, James Williams of Tadley, pulled his engines and rides near to Aldermaston Aerodrome, as James discovered the Ministry needed vehicles to help extend the runways and buildings. James purchased lorries especially for this work, also two of his engines were working there as well.

As it is not well documented what engines Williams' still owned during the war years, it is not possible to ascertain which engines took part in this work. However the family are documented here as taking part in war duties.

Thank you to Mr Steven Pugh for this information.

HARRY SYMONDS

Early on in the war, showman Harry Symonds was wintering at Ludgershall, Wiltshire. It was during this time he discovered vehicles were needed to clear land to build Lambourn Aerodrome, in Wiltshire. Harry had a 5-ton engine, Garrett no. 28079, *Pride of Devon* reg CR 6003. In 1942, he bought, from another showman, Fowler no 9501, reg. DW 2268, *Queen Alexandra.* This engine he later scrapped at Hardwick's yard in 1947. Whether both or just one engine worked at the aerodrome we do not know. We do know Harry drove the engine himself for this work.

Also working in the area on haulage was London showman Laffiat Roberts, with his steam Foden.

When the work was finished, towards the end of the war, Harry started to travel again with his Dodgems and Ark ride around the London area, where he opened under black-out restrictions for "Holidays At Home" fairs.

Thank you to Harry Symonds for helping with information.

SHE DID SOMETHING DIFFERENT

Nottingham Goose Fair, October 1936.
Road Locomotive Society collection.

Headway, fowler reg BE 8558 engine no 15117, was new in 1920 to J Jury and son of Laceby, Lincolnshire for haulage and threshing work.

In 1926 it was bought by showman James Hibble of Nottingham who converted it to fairground specification. He merged with fellow-showman Morney Mellor in 1930 and, from then on, *Headway* worked with the new firm known as Hibble & Mellor's. It was used to haul and power their Gallopers, Cakewalk, Swish, Dodgems and Razzle-Dazzle rides. During the war years, Hibble & Mellors remained open but chiefly with only their Dodgems and used their other engines for this.

Around 1941 *Headway* was used for a different purpose than our other engines; she was used to act as a road block at Red Hill, on the main Mansfield to Nottingham Road, in order to create a single flow of traffic. We are unsure why this busy road would need to be reduced to single-file traffic at this point, but the Authorities would have had their reasons, no doubt.

In the late 1940s, the engine was sold on to George Bettison of Nottinghamshire and entered preservation. When George Bettison died in late 50s, the new owner was Jack Hardy of Leeds. *Headway* is still with us today and is now residing in Kilrea, Ireland.

THE MYSTERY OF VANGUARD

Burrell 2342 was first owned in 1900 by the Harrogate Gas Company. You will note the small front wheels; this was to negotiate the narrow lanes in which it had to work.

Taken at Harrogate Gas works. *The Martin Hallows collection.*

Each year the gas works held a Gala day. One of its coal wagons was especially painted and seats fitted, so once a year Burrell 2342's duty was to tow the wagon at the gala giving children rides in the parade. Only about three years after this, what with the cost of running the engines and the locals complaining when engines passed their homes, the gas works decided to return to the horse and cart!

The engine entered showland use in 1910 when sold to showman H Crowther of Nottinghamshire. The next owner was Miles Jarvis of Chasetown, Staffordshire, who named it *Vanguard* and used the engine to power his ride. The next owner was John Evans of Brecon, who later sold it to James Edwards of Croydon to work with his Gallopers.

The children of showland, watch and learn from a very young age how everything is done. Little Jimmy Edwards had seen the men light the engine fire several times. One day, little Jimmy decided to light the fire himself. So he stacked some boxes to climb upon the engine and managed to light the fire first time. Unfortunately it was not the right time of day for the engine to be lit and the family came running when they realised smoke was coming from the engine.

Vanguard ***Burrell 2342, reg E 5380, taken Redhill 1934.***
R. Smith collection.

James Edwards had three engines and this is one of those stories we cannot prove as a requisition, however, it can be told what did happen although very little is known. It was a severe incident, as the Army arrived and took all three engines away, including their Packard car. The family did not know where the engines were taken and heard nothing of them for many years. Then, slowly over the years, they started to surface.

You will notice on the log sheet, *Vanguard* was taxed by James Edwards in 1939 in Croydon, then there is a gap of five years after the Army took her away. So where did *Vanguard* go? What work was it doing? Who was using it, a contractor, or did the Army keep her?

After the war in 1945, the first owner, since the Army took *Vanguard* away, was showman John Body of Maidstone, Kent, which is not that far away from the London Area. However, the engine number 2342 is not listed for working in the city.

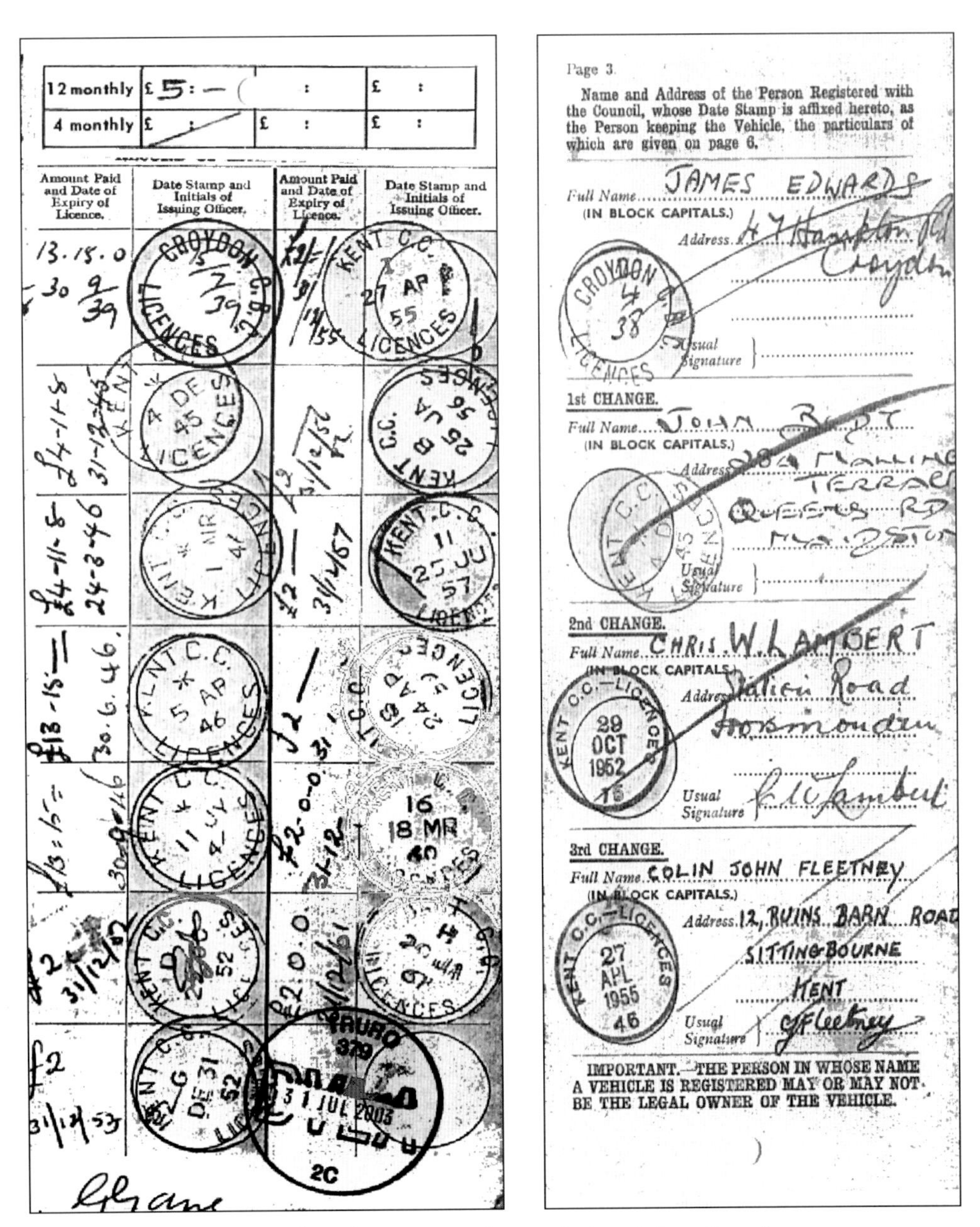

12 monthly	£ 5 : —	:	£ :
4 monthly	£ :	£ :	£ :

Amount Paid and Date of Expiry of Licence.	Date Stamp and Initials of Issuing Officer.	Amount Paid and Date of Expiry of Licence.	Date Stamp and Initials of Issuing Officer.
13.15.0 30 9/39	CROYDON C.B.C. LICENCES		KENT C.C. 27 AP 55 LICENCES
£4-1-8 31-12-45	KENT 4 DE 45 LICENCES	31/12/56	KENT C.C. 25 JA 56 LICENCES
£4-1-8 24-3-46	KENT 1 MR 46 LICENCES	£2 — 31/12/57	KENT C.C. 11 25 JU 57 LICENCES
£13-15 — 30.6.46	KENT C.C. 5 AP 46 LICENCES	£2 — 31	KENT C.C. 24 AP 49 LICENCES
£13-15 30-9-46	KENT C.C. 11 JY 46 LICENCES	£2-0-0 31-12	16 18 MR 40 LICENCES
£2 31/12/52	KENT C.C. 52 LICENCES	£2.0.0 31/12/51	LICENCES
£2 31/12/53	KENT C.C. DE 31 52 LICENCES	TRURO 379 31 JUL 2003 2C	

Page 3.

Name and Address of the Person Registered with the Council, whose Date Stamp is affixed hereto, as the Person keeping the Vehicle, the particulars of which are given on page 6.

Full Name. JAMES EDWARDS
(IN BLOCK CAPITALS.)
Address. 47 Hampton Rd Croydon
Usual Signature

1st CHANGE.
Full Name. JOHN BRITT
(IN BLOCK CAPITALS.)
Address. 18A MALLING TERRACE QUEENS RD MAIDSTONE
Usual Signature

2nd CHANGE.
Full Name. CHRIS. W. LAMBERT
(IN BLOCK CAPITALS.)
Address. Station Road Horsmonden
Usual Signature C.W. Lambert

3rd CHANGE.
Full Name. COLIN JOHN FLEETNEY
(IN BLOCK CAPITALS.)
Address. 12, RUINS BARN ROAD SITTINGBOURNE KENT
Usual Signature C J Fleetney

IMPORTANT.—THE PERSON IN WHOSE NAME A VEHICLE IS REGISTERED MAY OR MAY NOT BE THE LEGAL OWNER OF THE VEHICLE.

Note the dates on the original log book.
Courtesy of Robby Richards.

As the Army collected the engine from Croydon and then in 1945 it turned up in Kent, can we presume *Vanguard* may have remained in the South East area?

Vanguard's missing five years remain a secret which the engine will carry with her.

From the Roy Rice Archive.

This is *Vanguard* photographed not in the war years, but is a fine example of an engine using its winch. This was taken in the '60s when owned by Pegden Brothers of Elham, Kent.

The story goes that the Council tried to demolish the bridge, but failed, so Pegden's were ask to try with their engine, which it did with no problem.

In 1964, Eric Pegden decided to sell the engine and he advertised in the 'World's Fair' paper.

FOR SALE

For sale, 8 h.p D.C.C. Burrell Showmen's Engine,
Complete in all detail and on rubbers.

In good order. Pegden Bros, Elham, nr Canterbury, Kent.

Mr Jim Emerson of Banwell, nr Weston-Super-Mare, Somerset bought the engine from him for about £700.

Jim feeling proud.
From the Roy Rice archives.

From left to right: three members of the Edwards family, Eric Pincot, Jim Emerson and Tom Ridley. *From the Roy Rice archives.*

***Jim Emerson working on* Vanguard.** *From the Roy Rice archives.*

For 36 years it belonged to Jim Emerson. Jim took *Vanguard* to local rallies and the Bath & West Show. She was never on a low-loader, as Jim would drive her to all the events.

In 1973 *Vanguard* needed a pressure test, but Jim would not take the engine apart for this to be done, so the engine stood in a barn for 27 years. After his death in 2000, it was advertised for sale and in 2001 was bought by Robby Richards of Redruth, Cornwall, who did extensive work to the engine.

Robby working on the engine. *Photo from Robby Richards.*

Vanguard. *Photo courtesy of the Torbay Steam Fair.*

Thank you to all those who contributed to this story.

This is the second engine the Army collected from James Edwards.

Garrett Tractor* Mighty Atom *33305, reg HT 7112.
This photo was taken in New Malden, Surrey, July 1934.
Road Loco Society collection.

Built 1918 and sold to the Ministry of Munitions, then the next owner was David Harrison of Bristol, who converted it to a showmen's and travelled it with his Chair-o-Planes. In 1925 it was owned by James Edwards of Croydon, who named it *Mighty Atom.* When the Army took the engine away it is believed this engine did threshing for most of the war years. After the war the next owner was R Houchin of Billington, Kent.

The third engine to be taken was also a Garrett; *Olympic* built 1918, no, 33326 reg XO 8268. With inexperienced soldiers handling the engine, when collecting *Olympic,* it ended up going down a bank and part of the engine snapped. Although she was no good now for any work, the Army had orders to take the engine, so they did.

Like *Vanguard* it is a mystery as to what she did. This engine somehow survived, as later it belonged to showman J Penfold of Kent.

TIMBER & HAULAGE

A showmen's engine had to carry one 'C' licence for each trailer it towed, but the restriction with the 'C' licence was hauling showmen's goods only. You will now see showmen's engines were hauling not showmen's goods but timber on behalf of contractors, so the 'C' licences were made equal to 'A' licences, which meant engines could haul anything.

PETTIGROVE

Thomas Pettigrove of Stonebridge Park, London, was well-known around the Home Counties fairs travelling a set of steam gallopers with an 89-key Gavioli organ. He owned two engines: *Star,* Burrell no 3423, (that was laid up in his yard from 1938 and did not emerge until long after the war) and Foster no. 14501 reg. ND 983, *Victorious*, which Tom had purchased in 1920.

In 1929, Tom passed away and the engines were left to his sons, George and Dick Pettigrove.

In 1940, with the demand for haulage vehicles, they put *Victorious* on timber work around Gerrards Cross, in Buckinghamshire. However, it was soon found that the engine was not suitable for the task, being too heavy. Therefore, it was only used on war haulage for a short time. The spring gear was bent and it is thought the damage occurred when timber hauling in the forest.

The Pettigroves retained the engine in their other yard at Princes Risborough, near High Wycombe until 1985, before being bought for preservation.

Thank you to Sally Edmonds for helping with this information.

SYMONDS & COOK

By Philip Bradley. Copyright of The Surrey History Centre.

Burrell 3979, *Earl Haig* a 6 n.h.p. road loco, was new to W. J Taylor & Sons of Midsomer Norton in Somerset. In 1924 it entered showland by being sold to Mr & Mrs Edward Symonds of Gloucester, who rebuilt it as a showmen's and named it *Earl Haig,* after the famous WWI Army Commander.

By 1940, the Symonds had moved to Gillingham, Dorset to escape the bombing, where they remained for the war years and travelled locally, opening with their Ark ride. The family also decided in the winter months to put their engine on war work by pulling timber out from woodlands around the North Dorset area. Bernard Coles was also hauling timber with them and was using his Scammell lorry, which transported the wood to Hudson & Martins timber yard, in Poole.

It was during the war years that Edward Symonds passed away. However, Mrs Flo Symonds with her three children, kept everything going. In 1943, as *Earl Haig* being only a small 6 n.h.p., Flo Symonds decided to part with the engine.

Fred Darby & Sons of Ely, Cambridgeshire, were farm contractors and, with the demand for engines to do work of "National Importance", Fred purchased *Earl Haig.* Also, remember he acquired one of our previous engines, *Starlight* Burrell 3836 to meet the demand for threshing. So *Earl Haig* said 'goodbye' to the fairground and timber and went on to do work of "National Importance", by now doing threshing with Darby & Sons. *Earl Haig* certainly did her fair share of war work.

When Fred Darby finished working with *Earl Haig* she stood until 1964, by which time it was in a derelict state until bought by Mr Stan Burgess, who entered this engine into preservation.

When the Symonds family parted with *Earl Haig* in 1943, they replaced it with a larger engine, *Queen Mary* 8 n.h.p. Burrell 3833, which they purchased from the West Country showmen Anderton & Rowlands. *Queen Mary* was also put on timber work and remained with the Symonds family until 1950, when sold to Viv Kirk of Oxford, for preservation. *Queen Mary* is now in the Charles Burrell Museum, Thetford, Norfolk.

Both photos from Shane Seagrave.

Thank you to Mr George Symonds for helping with this information.

MURPHY'S TWO

Photo taken in a field at Inglewood Forest, Cumbria.

In May 1920, showman John Murphy of Gateshead, Co Durham, bought two engines from J. Fowler & Co, of Leeds, One was Fowler 15653, reg CU 978 and he named it *Renown.* The second engine was Fowler no 15652, reg CU 977 which he named *Repulse.* Both engines were fitted with 8" face flywheels and two injectors but had no brass twisted bars, stars or rings. These two engines travelled with Murphy's Proud Scenic Peacocks ride on the northern fairgrounds for twenty years.

F.H.T. collection.

With the outbreak of war, and the request for engines to work on the land, John put both *Renown* and *Repulse* on work of National Importance and were clearing wooded areas to create open land for food production. *Renown* went to Inglewood Forest, Cumbria. Some of the trees which were cleared went to "Swan Vesta" for matches. Meanwhile, *Repulse* worked in the Whitby area.

After the war *Renown* stood derelict at the showmen's yard at Houghton Le Springs. *Repulse* went to Tonks Haulers Yard at Wingate. Some time later *Renown* also went to Tonks Yard.

Renown *parked at Houghton Le Springs.*
By A. Scot. From Allan Downs collection.

In 1952, engine dealer "Parky Bates" wanted *Renown* for preservation, so he did a deal for the engine which was a complete swop for a new Gardner engine still in its wooden crate. In 1963 *Renown* was bought by Ran Hawthorn of Oxfordshire, who restored and rallied it with his sons.

On October 15th 1979, the engine was bought by Howard Bros of Derbyshire, who attended many rallies around the country with her.

In 2003 the engine was badly damaged when fire broke out in her storage area, so the Howard's restored the engine and have now owned it longer then anyone else.

Renown ***now in preservation.*** *From Allan Downs collection.*

MORE ABOUT REPULSE

As for *Repulse,* in 1956 Parky Bates returned to Tonks and purchased her, after which the engine had two more owners until coming into the ownership of Peter Startup in 1965. He owned the engine for 21 years, before it was purchased by the present owner in 1986. Over the next three winters it was completely overhauled by way of fitting a new canopy, tender, belly tanks, bearings and tyres. The dynamo was re-bushed and fitted on a new platform; the dynamo being made by Mather & Platt Ltd in 1927.

In 1993 *Repulse* won the trophy at the annual Dorset Steam Fair for working Billy Cole's Dodgems for 48hrs, generating between 300 and 350 amps continuously.

Repulse *Billinghurst 1960.*
From Allan Downs collection.

Thank you to showman Jimmy Cowie of Houghton Le Springs and also Mr Terry Gibson for this information.

TRY AGAIN

Allan Downs collection.

Burrell 3830, a 6 n.h.p., was new in March 1920 to showman Edwin Corrigan & Sons of Dewsbury, Yorkshire. The engine spent all its life on the fairgrounds with the Corrigan family, apart from in 1940, when the family answered the call and put the engine to work hauling timber. The engine was driven by Edwin's son, Johnny Corrigan, and worked around the Harrogate area.

Try Again *was working with their Ark before war was declared.*
From the National Fairground Archives, Sheffield.

Thank you to Mr Ron Dawe and Shaun Corrigan for this information.

KING CARNIVAL II

Stourpaine Bushes Rally, Saturday 22nd Sep 1979.
By H.C. From the Brian Burden collection.

King Carnival II was built 1932, reg EF 4883, a 10 n.h.p. showmen's, Fowler, no 19783. It was supplied to showman F.M Conville and travelled around Hartlepool, Co Durham. In 1941, engines were needed for war work and at that time the Conville family decided to let the engine go. It was sold and did war work by way of heavy haulage. The new licensee was then "Harp Wharf Cartage Co Ltd" who stripped the engine of all the showmen's fittings. The engine surfaced again in 1948, when sold to T. Cunliffe of Hansworth. He did not have the engine for many years, as in the 1950s it was sold to John Thompson, Boiler Makers of Wolverhampton and was used by them until 1968.

So this engine had a long working life before entering preservation. Now, with showmen's fittings replaced, this engine is on the rally fields as near as possible to its original condition.

MATTHEWS

Brothers Joe, John, Billy and Tommy Matthews of Emsworth, Hampshire, were open at Battle, nr Hastings, Sussex when war was declared. They remained open there with their fair until the end of the season, then they returned to their yard at Emsworth.

Soon engines were needed for timber haulage around the Portsmouth area and so, during the winter, two of their engines were working out of Horick's Timber yard.

By C. Durrant, copyright of Bill Brian.

Sunny South Burrell 3542 reg no 472. In 1929 it was bought by Charles Openshaw Ltd of Reading, who converted it to a showmen's, then that same year sold it to the Matthews'. This engine remained with the family until 1947, then was sold to J.Beach of Ashford, Middlesex, who worked the engine for 10 years before sending it to the scrap yard.

Bill Brian collection.

Fowler 13047 *Wanderer*, reg DP 3863 was built in 1914 as a road loco for the War Department. After the war, she belonged to Charles Openshaw, who converted the engine to a showmen's. This photo was taken May 27th 1940 at Shoreham Fair when in the ownership of the Matthews family. During the summer months the Matthews' remained open with their fair and returned her to timber hauling during the winter months. When the family were upgrading their transport in 1946, it was sold to Mr J.D. Foster. In the mid-1950s it went for scrap to Pollock & Co Ltd, Southampton.

Thank you to Mr George Matthews for helping with this information.

DEMOLITION IN THE CITIES

Apart from the engines working on the land, there were another group of engines doing their part for King and country. When the 'Blitz' started in September 1940, a little Army of showmen's engines took to the cities. Their job was DEMOLITION of bombed out buildings. These engines were desperately needed, so much so that some engines were brought out of retirement to work on the streets. Apart from London, Hitler's Luftwaffe targeted major cities such as Manchester, Plymouth, Birmingham, Liverpool and Swansea. Scotland's industrial areas suffered considerable damage as well.

WORKING WITH THE WINCH

Working in the cities, is where the showmen's engine's powerful winch proved to be invaluable. After the blitz on September 7th 1940, the cities were desperate to make the now high volume of damaged buildings safe. This is where the sheer strength of the engine's winch was put to use.

Liverpool. *Source unknown. (Thought to be from a film still).*

Here is an example of the high buildings the engines had to contend with. Above is one of our previous engines, Arthur Bates' *Her Majesty,*

Foster 3664. The driver was able to distance himself about 80 yards when winching, however it must have been a worrying experience with such height coming down and towards you, especially those who had already lost their canopy.

Previously we talked of the engines on timber haulage and airfield construction. When clearing land for food production or to create a runway, the winch was used to pull tree stumps and roots from the ground. The winch is located on the near side, behind the rear wheel. Here is a view of the winch drum and 'fairleads' – the steel rollers through which the rope is passed.

The length of the winch rope on each engine varied but averaged about 80 yards (73 metres).

***Example photo, engine* Earl Beatty.**

To activate the winch, the two cotter pins were removed, then the two drive pins were pulled out to disengage the road wheel. This now meant, through the action of the differential, the wheel drum could revolve without the wheel moving.

The rope would be pulled out between the winch guide rollers (fairleads) which guided the rope in either direction. (See over.)

***Fowler 14868* The Princess.** *Copyright Fox/Getty.*

Thank you to Nigel Myers, owner of General Gough *for helping with this information.*

MANCHESTER

On 22nd of December 1940, Manchester suffered its first severe attack by Hitler's Luftwaffe. At 6.37pm the sirens sounded and within two minutes landmines, bombs and incendiaries were raining down on an almost defenceless city. In the next two hours 560 fires were burning throughout Manchester and much of the city had been reduced to rubble. On December 23rd, at 7.12pm, the sirens wailed again for a second attack. 441 Luftwaffe aircraft struck the city again. At 1.23am the all clear sounded.

37,150 incendiaries had fallen over the two nights (15 hours of bombardment) and 1077 bombs, 95 landmines and 170 flares. 576 civilians were dead and nearly 2,000 injured. Over the two days it was recorded as the biggest blaze since the Great Fire of London in 1666. All over the city there were unsafe walls of burnt-out buildings and the remaining walls had to come down.

And this is where *J.P. COLLINS* enters the story...

The Collins engine, **King George VI.** *A.J. Martin.*

The Collins Fowler 9487* King George VI, *pulling down the Victoria Hotel, Manchester. The two stone blocks behind each wheel would help hold her back when winching.

The second engine he had on demolition work was Foster 14263 *Roosevelt* reg HR4186 and was named after Teddy Roosevelt the US President.

Hightown, Manchester.
By 'The Cyclist'.

Roosevelt, for a short while, had been working at the Foden works at Sandbach, Cheshire where they were extending their premises to accommodate war work. They had no hot water boiler, so all *Roosevelt* was needed for was its boiler and not the machinery. Her dynamo was made by 'Royce,' a Manchester engineering firm, who later partnered with Rolls.

Roosevelt was on demolition work for only a short time in Manchester.

***Foster,* Roosevelt.** *Photo supplied by Brian Collins.*

James' brother, M.A. Collins, had two engines which both only worked on the fairground. This is *Clara,* Foster 13052, reg DH 2477.

Clara *at Ashton Under Lyme.* *J. Palmer.*

She did help out, for one week only, on demolition when *King George VI* was having repairs carried out at an engineering firm in Chester.

Two showmen who were earning a living by driving for J.P. Collins were Walter Holland and Jack Gill. Walter Holland was seriously hurt in a wire rope accident, caused by one of the Maiden employees not fastening the rope properly.

Kevin Collins described the work as: *"A good job at the time and it was money coming in."*

20/8/41

FUN FAIRS AID BLITZED

The men behind the Manchester's blitz clean up are saying "thank you" to the fairground kings.

It sounds odd, but it's true, that the machines used to drag down buildings and clear up bomb sites have been traction engines from the fairgrounds.

The power in peace time that drives the Round a bouts and Dodgems has played a decisive part in ironing out bomb damage. Demolition men hope to have the job completed around the City in 8 weeks.

Both *King George* and *Roosevelt* never returned to showland as the sites they worked on were extremely rough and it took its toll on the engines. After their work a member of the family described them as a wreck. With diesel power now taking over, both engines were taken to the scrap yard and sold for £5 each.

The dynamo on *King George VI,* which was a 200 amp made by Mather & Platt, was removed and put on an Armstrong Saurer diesel tractor.

Roosevelt ***14263 and*** **King George VI** ***9487 working together unaware of the work they would later be doing, then only to be scrapped.*** *From the Collins collection.*

One particular night Manchester sustained heavy bombing and the Vehicle Taxation building was bombed beyond repair. Only one side was remaining, with its high gable end. Much discussion went on between the Chief of Police and the Fire Officer before pulling it down. The engine's name doing the job is not known, however, all we know is it was a showmen's which had no canopy and belonged to the Collins family. With a wire rope attached to the building the driver pulled slowly forward pulling the structure towards him. The driver was on his own at the time and had to dodge about so that the falling masonry missed him. The building came down but unfortunately burst a water main.

Mr S D Rudd, Chief of the Manchester Architects building staff, told a national news paper:

> *"The traction engines had done a great deal to help. We were the first city to use these engines for demolition work, others have followed our example. It was a lucky day when Mr Collins, fairground owner put this suggestion to us."*

SAMUEL INGHAM

***8 n.h.p. Burrell* William V.** *Photo by S. Love.*

Another family who put their engine on war duty, were the Inghams, from Cheshire. Pat, daughter of Samuel Ingham, has kindly provided information about her family.

William V, built 1914, Burrell no 3610, was new to showman William Murphy, of Durham, who named the engine after himself. Next it passed to his son Thomas Murphy then, in 1933, it was sold it to Samuel Ingham to work with his Dodgems.

In 1941 Sam put this engine on demolition in Manchester. Both Sam Ingham and his brother-in-law, Edward (Teddy) Morley were working with the engine. Sam decided to join the Royal Observer Corp and Teddy continued working with the engine. Sam retained *William V* and in 1951 sold it to fellow showmen J Botton & Sons of Croydon.

Stood here in Botton's yard.
Photo by Barry J. Finch.

In 1955, life was about to start all over again for this engine, as Mr J Kingdom, of Reading purchased the engine but did little work to it.

The next owner was Mr John Crawley. When in his ownership stardom came her way. In 1963 she starred alongside Fowler 15657 *Kitchener* which was re-named *The Iron Maiden* in the film of the same name. *William V* also changed names to *Dreadnought.* Her preservation paint work was replaced by 'battleship grey' and, as this was only temporary for the filming, the lining on her was made from adhesive tape.

Filming. *From the John Crawley collection.*

Filming took place outside the Pinewood studio house. This is where the driver used for filming, lost control and *William V* ran away hitting a tree branch! The canopy was smashed and was repaired by the studio's wood shop, which did an excellent job.

After filming, she was painted back to her preservation colours and is still admired on the rally fields today.

HARNIESS OF DONCASTER

Another family who played an important part in work of National importance were the Harniess's of Doncaster. Frank Harniess was open with his fair under blackout covers in the centre of Doncaster. At the same time he had three of his engines on war duties. Over the years he had about 14 engines in his ownership. Looking at the dates he parted with his engines, we have narrowed it down to three still in his ownership,

Perseverance II	Burrell 3483
Sir Douglas Haig	Foster 14401
Jubilee	Fowler 9180

His grandson, Frank Harniess, believes the engines took part in threshing, timber and demolition work in and around the Doncaster area.

WALES – HENRY STUDT

Burrell no 3948 *John Bull* was new in 1923 to Henry Studt of South Wales. After WWI the name was changed to *Kitchener* but we will still refer to this engine as *John Bull.* As there is no photo of this engine, here are a few details about it; the rear wheels were 7ft in diameter, which would have made it a little faster on the road, and had forward roping pulleys, one on the front tank and one on the smoke box. The steam chest covers were lagged and covered with brass cladding on which there were embossed dragons.

After the last job *John Bull* did, she was taken to Clydach and covered over with corrugated iron for protection, then only to be scrapped in 1958.

Reported in the 'World's Fair' by 'The Bard' 6/9/41:

> Henry Studt of the South Wales section, following the 3 night blitz on Swansea in February last, the engines 'John Bull' and 'King George' were immediately on the job of street clearing and have been among the debris ever since.

***Above is the engine that worked along side* John Bull,**
King George V, *Fowler 11826, reg CY 4360.*
Photo from the Road Loco Society.

Photo from a book of memories, source unknown.

The picture bottom of p.64 is either Danter's Burrell 3590 *Kitchener* or *John Bull.* The photo is taken at such distance, that it can not be agreed as to which engine it is.

No photos of the *John Bull* can be found, so this could be a rear photo of it seen here working amongst the rubble in Swansea, which suffered extensive bombing in 1941.

The photo below was also taken at some distance in Swansea in Jan/Feb 1941. We are unsure if this is a Henry Studt engine, but you can see how minute these engines looked among such devastation.

EARL KITCHENER

Burrell no 3590 *Kitchener* reg NC 2250 was new to a showman mentioned earlier in this book, J.P. Collins, of Liverpool. It attended their Orton & Spooner Scenic Motors along with engine *Roosevelt* (also mentioned earlier). In 1930 J. Collins no longer used the engine and so it was sold to showmen Danter & Sons of Newport, who not only used the engine for travelling but, in 1941, put the engine to work on the Swansea Blitz demolition work.

HAMPSHIRE SHOWMAN

Photo by B.D. Stoyel.

Old Bill, a Fowler B6 compound engine no 9295, reg CU 913 was built in 1902 for the War Dept. It was one of ten built with a long fire box for oil burning. We know it was in the ownership of showman Maurice Stokes, of Basingstoke by 1929 and was named after Maurice's grandfather, William Stokes, (Old Bill). This engine will be one of four owned by this showman.

Endurance. *From the Len Crane collection.*

Endurance Burrell 2547 was new to J.K. Cooper brickworks, based at Maidenhead, Berkshire. Ten years later it was owned by Charles Prior, who used *Endurance* for timber haulage during WWI.

In 1933, showman Sam Stokes and his son Maurice, acquired *Endurance* for £60. They sent the engine, for conversion to a showmen's, to Wallis & Stevens Ltd, of Basingstoke.

Also that same year they purchased a 5 ton Burrell tractor no 3631, which was built in 1915 for showman W. Gritt of Romsey, and called Pride of Romsey. The Stokes family renamed her *Bluebird.*

Bluebird. *By B.D. Stoyel.*

267 Reg: No AH.0225. ↑ on Smoke-box

NAME OF ENGINE :— PRIDE OF ROMSEY — Made up to order 4116.

5 Ton Double Crank Comp: 3 Speed Double Geared Spring Tractor. ENGINE NHP. — Sent away to order 2898. — No. 3631

For W. Griff. Romsey. Premium Mfg Co ordering part for this tractor. M Stokes Basingstoke

Sent away Jan: 4th 1915.

Cylinders 4½ & 4½" Stroke 8½" Steam Pressure 200.

Grate Area 3 Fire Box Surface 14.25 Tube Surface 48.25. Total 65.5.

Road Gear 3 Speeds 24.4 to 1 and 13.64 to 1 and 7.43. to 1.

Driving Wheels 5'-0½" Diameter 12" Wide. Over width as measured on Engine. 5'-7½"

Leading „ 3'-0" „ 5. „ „ „

ROAD GEAR.	Pitch.	Wide.	No. of Teeth	Material.	Marks.	Remarks.		key ways
First Pinion, Slow	1⅛	1⅞"	16	Steel.	L.3063.	2¾ bore	8	
„ „ Intermediate	„	1 11/16"	25		L.3064.	„ „	„	„
„ „ Fast	„	1½"	37		L.3433.	10¾ „	„	„
„ Spur, Slow	„	1¾"	41		L.3065.			
„ „ Intermediate	„	„	62					
„ „ Fast	„	1½"	50		L.3446			
Differential Pinions	1¼"	2"	10		L.4007			
„ Wheel fixed	„	„	30		L.4009.			
„ „ loose	„	„	30					
Main Spur Pinion & Bevel Wheel	1¾	2¼"	12		L.4177.			
Main Spur Pinion	„	„	12		L.3059		2⅞" bore.	
„ Spur R.H. / L.H.	„	„	66 / 66		L.3058 / L.3057			

GUN METAL FITTINGS.

Dewrance Water Gauge No 31. 10 centres Glass 8" long { Top bracket L.3194. Bottom bracket } of hydraulic piping.

Boiler Test Cock No 192.

Mansell D.A. pump. Lubricator on Steam Chest — Whistle 1¼ Organ.

2 Cocks on Tank No 72. — Blow-off Cock

Straight way asbestos packed gland Cylinder Drain Cocks No 109.

½ Cock for Water Lifter Stephens' screwdown valve No 265 fixed on R.H. side of cylinder.

¾ Steam Cocks for Injectors . . . . . — No 255

½ Suction „ „ „ No 84.

½ Blower Cock Stephens straight way valve No 254.

Cutler Pressure Gauge 5". Marked to 300 lbs, red line at 200 lbs.

Detail Reference Book No. 23 *Pages.* 201 to 208.

Weight.	Front.	Hind	Total.
Empty	1-8.0.	4.12.2.	6.0.2.

Weighed in one piece 6. 0. 2.

Complete with & painted Long Awning, Wire Rope, Tools & Anchors.

***This is the specification sheet for* BlueBird *which was originally known as* Pride of Romsey.**

You may think three engines were more than ample for a small-time showman but, the Stokes family needed the engines to travel with their Chair-o-Planes and three-abreast gallopers, which were built by Savages of Kings Lynn, Norfolk. Also, during the winter months, the family undertook haulage as a second income.

In March 1939, five months before the declaration of war, Sam Stokes died and his eldest son Maurice, at the age of 55, became head of the family. His other son, James had left the family to travel on his own so Billy (41), Robert (42), and Tusher (39) all worked within the business, keeping everything on the road.

The family remained open with their fair during the war years by operating their equipment under blackout covers. In 1939, Maurice increased his transport by acquiring yet another engine, *Queen of The Road,* a Wallis & Stevens 4 n.h.p. compound oil-bath tractor no 7393, reg AA 5126. This engine was converted to a showmen's and was re-named *Nobby.*

From Road Loco Society.

On August 4th 1939, when travelling through Shrewton, nr Salisbury, Wiltshire and just one month before war commenced, *Endurance's* front axle broke.

By Futcher.

One month later, on September 7th, war was declared. The engine had been repaired and the travelling season was coming to an end. Then there was the demand for transport to come forward for war work. So, as in previous winters, Maurice continued to work the engines.

The firms they worked for were:

- E.C. Whites – wood timber merchants on the site of the old Basingstoke canal wharf.
- Wallis & Stevens Traction Engine Engineers, (moving coal).
- The Southern Railway Co, Basingstoke station.

On the occasion when the centre of Basingstoke suffered heavy bombing, their engines assisted in clearance and demolition work. After the war, they also were involved in clearing the huge anti-tank concrete blocks placed around the town.

When the work was finished, the Ministry who hired the engines for the work gave Maurice a certificate, so he could now take the engines for any repairs needed caused by doing the demolition work. As it happen *Endurance's* firebox needed attention and it went to Wallis & Stevens for the work to be done. *Endurance* was retired in 1952, and stood alongside *Bluebird* for the next four years, both engines deteriorating fast due to their hard working past.

Photo by David Hunt.

From the Ron Dawe collection.

In 1956 Mr David Hunt of Sherborne, Dorset, bought *Endurance* for preservation. Mr Hunt rallied the engine for a little while, until the rear axle broke.

Photo by David Hunt.

The engine then stood on a farm until 1989, when bought as a birthday present for himself by Mr Len Crane of Wolverhampton, who has carried out extensive restoration work to the engine.

Bluebird remained in the Stokes family yard for a further three years, then, in March 1958, it was sold to Mr Jack Laurence of Great Milton, Oxfordshire.

It was not steamed but towed home at a steady 4 mph by an American LHD Ex-WWII military vehicle. The engine was in a poor state and the canopy was rotten, with the top boards falling off at regular bumps in the road. The chimney too was taken off to save further damage as the base casting fell apart.

Jack, along with his son, Allan, worked on the engine until she was fully restored. *Bluebird* was renamed *Kathleen.* The nameplate came from an agricultural engine used locally for threshing, etc, and driven by a character named "Jimmer" Mason. When "Jimmer" retired, the engine was eventually scrapped by a local showman, Victor Farr. However, he saved the nameplate and put it in a toolbox in a Tillings Stevens lorry.

When Jack Lawrence bought *Bluebird* he did not want to paint it blue or revert to its original name of *Pride of Romsey.* Victor told Jack, "I will give you the nameplate *Kathleen* if you put it on your engine and not put it on a wall." This Jack promised to do. *Kathleen* was Jack's pride and joy and he was sad to part with her in 1990. The engine is now in the ownership of Kevin Gamlen of Bristol.

Nobby was eventually sold to showman Harry Symonds of London.

Thank you to Len Crane, Allan Lawrence and 'Fairs & Markets of Basingstoke' published 2000 by Steven Pugh.

PLYMOUTH

7 n.h.p. Burrell, no 3159, reg CO 3823.
From the Road Locomotive Society archive.

The Gladiator was built 1909 for West Country showmen Anderton & Rowlands. Originally she worked beside engines 2471 *John Bull* and *The Showman,* 2716 and later was used with the Venetian Gondolas.

From A&R family collection.

In 1932, *The Gladiator* was sold to showman Tommy Whitelegg, so it continued to travel around the West country fairs. Throughout the war Tommy's amusements were open in a building called Olympia in Union Street, Plymouth. *The Gladiator* was parked alongside the building supplying power to the Dodgems, Ark and stalls.

In 1940, Plymouth was suffering heavy bombing, and the coastal defences would fire at the oncoming enemy planes trying to bring them down before reaching land. But, of course, most got through our defences. When the enemy reached land the guns would fall silent, as bringing down a plane fully laden would cause a bigger explosion over a wide area and cause more damage. Therefore Plymouth could only watch helplessly as thousands of tons of explosives rained down on them, leaving heaps of rubble and sheer devastation. Bombs landed close to the Olympia but the building and *The Gladiator*, thankfully, both escaped damage.

Around this time, Tommy Whitelegg decided to put a diesel generator next to the building to supply the power, therefore *The Gladiator* was no longer needed.

In 1941, Plymouth desperately needed help clearing the rubble and to demolish unsafe buildings left by the raids. So, for a short time Tommy allowed *The Gladiator* to do work of National importance by demolition in and around the city of Plymouth.

When in 1941, Hitler turned his attentions to Russia, the bombing petered out and *The Gladiator* returned to the Whitelegg's yard in Exeter. Tommy then discovered engines were needed for timber haulage, so he teamed together *The Gladiator* and his other engine, *King of the Belgians,* a 6 n.h.p. Burrell no 3711 reg TA 3067. Both engines went on timber haulage at Holden Hill, between Plymouth and Exeter. However, when soldiers saw the name plate, *King of the Belgians* they asked the family to cover the plate.

Copyright of Barry J. Finch.

After the evacuation of Dunkirk, in 1940, the King of Belgium requested an Armistice with Germany. He did not consult his government about this and consequently, Hitler completed his conquest of France and Belgium. As **the King of Belgium** had capitulated, everyone condemned his actions and demanded that he abdicate. It was even worse in November 1940 when the King actually met with Adolf Hitler. After that people saw him as a collaborator. **Therefore the name plate on the engine was covered as a mark of respect.**

After the war the engines were no longer needed, so they were taken back to the yard, where both needed boiler testing, to make them legal for the road. They were taken to Hodgsons for the test, where one failed. This was put right and both were eventually sold. *The Gladiator* was bought in 1953 by the newly-formed The Gladiator Club, who used the engine to take the famous Anderton & Rowland Marenghi organ around West Country rallies, raising money for charity.

Redruth Fairfield 1958. *Photo supplied by Peter Phillipps.*

Photo supplied by Mr David Goodwin.

Taken in September 1953, at Taylors mine shaft at East Pool. The mine's head-gear had collapsed and *The Gladiator* winch was used to pull down the remainder.

After 32 years, in 1985 with much work needed doing to the engine, it was then bought by David Goodwin of Cornwall, who has carried out extensive work such as the firebox, boiler barrell, front tube plate, smoke box and various bearings.

MORE ABOUT *KING OF THE BELGIANS*

From the Whitelegg family collection.

Weight 17 tons, built 1916 and, when new, was bought by Melhuish Transport Contractors of Chard, Somerset. In 1922, the next owner was West Country showman Tommy Whitelegg. This engine was the first Tommy bought.

He travelled *King of the Belgians* around Devon, Cornwall and Somerset fairs. After doing timber work at Holden Hill the engine was parked in Tommy's yard, at Exeter, along with *The Gladiator.*

In 1953 enthusiast Dennis Chappell of West Buckland, Somerset purchased *King of the Belgians*, then in 1970 it was bought by Mr C.J. Lee, who rallied the engine for two years then placed it in the Country Life Museum, Exmouth.

You will note, both engines have spent all their life in the West Country.

LONDON

The Showmen as young boys had experience on the engines from driving them around the fair field then, when older, progressing to the road. That is why a number of showmen, too old to fight, found work driving on the London streets. London showman Pepper Biddall did not have engines himself in the city, however he was working by driving various engines for the showmen.

With the country's resources stretched to the limit, engine enthusiast Philip Bradley reported his first sighting of a showmen's engine in London, October 4th 1941. However, demolition work must have started before this, taking into consideration the blitz started in September 1940.

Bradley would tour the blitzed areas of the city in the company of Tom Pearce of Cambridge and on one day alone they found 17 engines, 13 of them being of Showmen's type. Philip Bradley would note down in a little book every engine he came across, including the date, name, number and owner. This publication has found and accounted for every showmen's engine on Bradley's London list, plus others he did not find.

THERE IS SOMETHING YOU SHOULD BEAR IN MIND WHEN READING ABOUT THE FOLLOWING ENGINES.

When the day's work was done the engines were parked up in the city ready for the following morning. Between 1940 and 1942 the cities were experiencing heavy bombing. It's as though these engines were on the front line, as at night the bombs were raining down around them. Men arriving for work each morning must have wondered what they were going to find. You will read later how two of the Botton engines were victims of enemy bombing and men working on engine *General Gough* also had a surprise one morning.

DEMOLITION

June 5th 1942.

Above is Fowler 13152, reg TA 635. It travelled with John Sander's Chair-o-planes around the London and Middlesex fairs for many years. It is well known this is a Fowler, however, it has been noted that no makers plate could be seen on the engine.

On October 18th 1941, Philip Bradley spotted this engine working on the streets of London. This is the only engine John Sanders had working on demolition. This is a sad sight (above) of this Fowler after falling into a cellar in Queen Victoria Street, London, near St Paul's. The dynamo broke free and ended up lodged in the canopy, but fortunately the driver was not seriously hurt. Charles Abbot was nearby with his engine and helped John Sanders climb out and away from the engine. The engine was also salvaged with help from Fowler 14916 *Demolicious* which was being driven by fellow showman Charles Abbot.

From a different angle.
Both Photos by B.D. Stoyel.

This happened towards the end of her duties in 1942 and she was seen again by Bradley June 13th 1942, the same year the demolition ended and John Sanders put the engine up for sale. The next owner was showman Bert Ayres of Uxbridge, who did not own the engine long, as he re-sold it on to Syd Smart of Wealdstone, Middlesex.

Bill Brian collection.

Here she is again, Fowler 13152 in the ownership of Syd Smart. Now re-painted and the name *Spitfire* painted on her, which is the name the engine is mostly associated with. Syd also fitted a Holmes dynamo in 1943 as, previously, J. Sanders had removed the original.

In 1944 the engine was up for sale again:

'World's Fair' news paper 4/11/1944

For sale, 7 h.p. 3 speed Fowler, fitted full cab, dynamo plate, pump and injector, good rubber, good order. Reasonable offers accepted. Reason for selling, no further use.

Syd Smart, Fairground, Canning Road, Wealdstone.

John Body of Maidstone, Kent bought the engine, but only used it for a year, and is now presumed scrapped.

ILLUMINATOR

From the late Ernie Taylor collection.

Fowler 13469 built 1914, reg DP 4392, was new to the War Department. It is thought this engine severed abroad when new, as she was not registered for the road until 1922. The same year the War Department had a clear out and sold her and her sister engines (consecutive numbers) at Staple Bros, Auctions. It was bought by Charles Openshaw and he converted it to a showmen's and named it *Illuminator.* In 1923, he then sold it to the Butlin family of West Drayton, Middlesex. The engine travelled with the Chair-o-planes and belonged to Miss Charlotte Butlin. Philip Bradley reported seeing *Illuminator* at Kingsbury Fete in North West London on July 14th 1937. It had extra brass work added in 1938. Two years later, in 1940, it was bought by Syd Squires who put this engine on demolition duties.

It was seen on the London streets by Philip Bradley on October 11th 1941 and last spotted November 9th 1942. We are unsure if this one went back to the fairground after the war, however, we do know it was one of the last engines working in the city and then scrapped in 1950.

MAUDE

London showman J. Rose's engine,* Maude *Foster, no 3642, reg PB 9832. *By Philip Bradley. Copyright of Surrey History Centre.*

In 1908, a contractor named Dagnall, ordered a new foster engine and he named it *Maude* after his daughter. Then Jack Rose of London, purchased *Maude* in 1911, at an auction in Hendon, London.

Enthusiasts reported it missing in 1938. Two years later at Easter 1940, it was seen again, newly painted in dark blue with red wheels and lined in silver. It looked a picture!

The photo above was taken by enthusiast Philip Bradley March 22nd 1940. He spotted the engine again October 4th 1941 towing small trailers of rubble and masonry which was being cleared from the roads, so allowing transport to continue to flow. Bradley reported in his note book, that:

"The city work had spoilt the fine finish of her paintwork."

Maude also did work in WWI, so this was not a new experience for the Rose family. Jack Rose drove the engine himself by day, then would drive back to Maidenhead to open each night with his Dodgems. On one occasion an incendiary bomb went through the top of his Dodgems but, thankfully did not go off. *Maude* finished work in the city about 1942.

Maude is still owned by the Rose family.

Photo from Fred Rose.

ARTHUR TRAYLEN

Arthur Traylen senior, from Earlsfield, London, stayed open with his rides in and around the London area throughout the war. He would move to High Wycombe when the bombing became too severe, then return to London when things had quietened down again.

Arthur also purchased two steam Fodens, no 8416 reg N 9714 and no 1120, reg N 1182 to help move his rides. This was because Arthur's traction engines were helping with the demolition work.

Marina. *Photo by B.D. Stoyel.*

Burrell 2576, reg KE 5879 he had on demolition work in the city. Arthur converted this engine to a showmen's and named it *Marina.* He also had Foster 14381 *Queen Mary*, reg CL 4318 which, we believe, did some demolition work for a short time. In 1941, *Queen Mary* was photographed back on the fairground at Uxbridge.

The engines were not given to a demolition contractor, instead Arthur and his brother George and engine driver, Frank Seaton, did the work themselves. However, Arthur did not like driving the engine, so the job was given to George and Frank.

As the engines would clear a bombed site, Arthur would ask for his fair to open on the now cleared land. He would stay there for a number of weeks and then, as another site was cleared, he moved to that one but was still opening between times with Irvin's fair. After the war both engines were parked in the family yard at Feltham, as the family were upgrading their transport to lorries. In June 1950, the engines were sold on for £100 to Hardwick's scrap yard. *Marina* was cut up in Hardwick's yard that same year.

Thank you to Arthur Traylen for this information.

MARVEL

William Irvin's Foster* Marvel *7 n.h.p. no 12499 reg HO 5702.
Philip Bradley. Copyright the Surrey History Centre.

William Irvin 1859-1917.
The Irvin collection.

William Irvin and wife Harriet, during the early years, travelled with a small steam dobby set (Round-a-bout). The young couple experienced many ups and downs, in some cases with bankruptcy not far away.

Harriet Irvin with daughters Lily, Ada and Florence.
Irvin collection.

Life progressed and in 1904 William bought a set of gallopers from T Danter of Swansea. Eventually, in 1910, George could afford the engine *Marve*l by way of part exchange for engine *William the*

Conqueror. He said it was "a bloody marvel" how he paid for it, hence he named the engine *Marvel*! As business improved, in 1916 William bought a second engine, a brand new Foster, *Marvellous* an 8 n.h.p. no 14057, reg HO 5701.

In WWI, William put both his engines at the disposal of the military; whether they were requisitioned we are unsure. Nevertheless, William remained with his engines by driving them himself.

On November 26th 1917, William was working on a Government contract at a sawmill in Cobham, Surrey. *Marvellous* was lifting timber when a tree slipped from the sling and crushed him. He died instantly. His young son, George, was driving the engine at the time and lived with the terrible memory of the accident for the rest of his life.

Marvellous *Mitcham Common 2/4/42.*
By Philip Bradley. Copyright the Surrey History Centre.

After the war, *Marvellous* was loaned to another showman and, for years, the engine had a geared up dynamo, which eventually burnt out. It was replaced with an ordinary substitute, but this also burnt out. After this the engine stood at Hendon for a while, until George Irvin went to collect it, only to find it had not been drained of water, so it had stood for two winters with the boiler full! After a few minor repairs, *Marvellous* steamed well and went back on the road.

With William now having passed away, in 1939 George continued to improve the business. He bought a new speedway ride, which *Marvellous* was used to power. Meanwhile, war was declared with the blitz taking its toll in London.

In 1940 *Marvel* returned to war work again by doing demolition in the City of London. Some walls were so thick they were difficult to bring down, so a snatch block was used on the winch rope for a double pull. *Marvel* was seen by Bradley working on the October 18th 1941 and again on November 9th 1941. George remained open with the fair at Hounslow then travelled into the City each day. He would take his twin sons, Billy and Benny, along and although only about 9 years old, they were allowed to steer the engine for a little while. When the bombing subsided, *Marvel* returned to the fairgrounds in 1942.

She was describe as a handsome engine, with yellow wheels, twisted brass, brass beading and stars and rings on the motion covers. She also carried a brass steering wheel.

Marvel was always the family favourite. Seen here with George are, his Nephews, young Arthur and George Traylen.

Both engines went for scrap for £25 each

GENERAL GOUGH

From the Nigel Myers collection.

General Gough an 8 n.h.p. Burrell, engine no 3888, was bought new by showman Swales Bolesworth of London. She remained in the Bolesworth family being later owned by Henry and Tom Bolesworth. She was used during the war years to clear bombed sites within the London area.

On one occasion, after a long hard day pulling down the remains of unsafe buildings, the men parked the engine up for the night on a newly cleared site but, unknown to them, the engine was standing over underground cellars. When the men returned the following morning they discovered that, during the night, the engine had fallen through the ground into a cellar. She was so far down the men could walk across the top of the canopy.

Above story from the Late Ernie Taylor.

After the war, General Gough returned to the fairgrounds, but now steam on the fairs was slowly coming to an end. General Gough left showland and was later acquired by scrap merchant Jesse Vines. In the early 50s she was sold to steam enthusiast Viv Kirk of Oxford, then in 58/59 was purchased by Jimmy Miller of Bristol, who stored and rallied General Gough for many years.

***Peter Parrish and the late Ernie Taylor with* General Gough.**
From the Parrish collection.

How deep?

We have mentioned an underground cellar. As the bombing weakenened the ground, here is an example of the problem the engines had. Also, eye witnesses have said engines were seen lifting/ dragging iron girders from deep holes within the ground.

JAMES BOTTON SENIOR

Both father and son of the Botton family had engines in the city on demolition but, unfortunately it was not for long for James Botton senior.

James Botton had acquired two engines from showman Jimmy Sanders. The Bottons never travelled with these two engines and both were parked away in the Botton's yard at Croydon. Therefore the change of ownership has not been recorded; due to this the names of these engines cannot be traced. When, in 1940, engines were needed for the City, as these two engines were stood idle in the yard, James returned to Croydon to collect them and put them to work on demolition. Each day he would work on the engines, taking his young son, Albert, along to watch. They had only been working for about three weeks when they had an unfortunate ending. The engines had been working on a factory which had been badly bombed, in Farringdon Road, near Smithfield Market. At the end of the day, as usual, both engines were parked up for the night and James went home.

But during 1940 and 41, London was experiencing heavy bombing and, during an air raid one night, one engine took a direct hit and the blast destroyed them both. The family contacted Jack Hardwick at West Ewell, Surrey who was buying any engines that came his way. So Hardwick collected them both for scrap and that was the end of demolition work for James Botton Snr.

Thank you to Albert Botton for supplying this information.

JAMES BOTTON JNR

Enterprise 6 n.h.p. Burrell, no 3311 reg KE 3862.
Photo from R. Smith.

New in 1911 and during its lifetime had several owners within Showland. Jimmy Botton (son of the above) was one. He used it in the city for demolition work and we believe he was driving the engine himself. Philip Bradley reported seeing the engine working November 29th 1941, then again on June 13th 1942. When the work ended, Enterprise returned to the fairgrounds under new owners; Walls Bros, of Petersfield, Hampshire. It was finally scrapped in 1950.

From R. Smith collection.

Jimmy's second engine was Little Edward 6 n.h.p. Burrell, no 3604, reg KE 3893. This photo was taken in April 1938. It was new in 1914, to W. Arnold of Kent. This engine served in both world wars, before eventually going to London showman Jimmy Botton. In 1940, he put the engine to work in London. It was seen by Philip Bradley November 9th 1941, he never reported seeing it again but it is known she returned to the fairground in 1942, still in the ownership of J Botton. It was eventually scrapped at Hardwick's yard.

R HEWITT

Allan Downs collection.

Fowler 15324, reg ME 8546 *Renown*, was seen by enthusiast Philip Bradley March 10th 1942 and again June 13th 1942. We do not think this one returned to the fairgrounds after the work was done.

Another engine owned by R Hewitt was seen by Bradley November 9th 1941, but we are unable to identify it due to a lack of information. All that can be said is it was a Fowler engine, which was seen on the fairground by Philip Bradley in 1936. Now it was working under B&G transport and was not reported on a fairground again.

Sometimes the showmen did not name their engines and Bradley noted in his book, that there were times like above, when it was advisable to keep a safe distance and sacrifice obtaining an engine number, due to falling masonry.

MINORU

Mrs A Brown of Surrey, had an 8 n.h.p. Wallis & Stevens engine no 7130, reg HT 3796. This was taken May 6th 1939 at Guildford. With war not declared yet, when pictured here, little did the family know in four months we would be at war.

The proposed first owner could not take delivery of this one so, instead, was new to Bristol showmen Marshall and Ernest Hill, then was sold to Mrs Brown in 1934. In 1941, she sold the engine to showman J Biddall, of B&G Transport, who used the engine for demolition in London. Philip Bradley reported seeing the engine October 18th 1941. It is not known if *Minoru* returned to the fairgrounds after the work but, what we do know is the engine ended her days at Hardwick's scrap yard at West Ewell.

FAIRWAY

From the J. Crawley collection.

Philip Bradley spotted Foden tractor 13250, *Fairway* reg WN 334, working on the streets of London October 18th 1941. What caught Bradley's eye was the flywheel on the off-side. It was last seen doing demolition work, March 10th 1942. It formerly belonged to showman Mr Phil Case, of Swansea. Then he sold it to London County Council War Debris Survey Committee, who numbered it 424 in their fleet.

H Sabey & Co, Ltd handled the engines for the County Council. Bradley said:

"The tractor was fitted with a dynamo on the usual smoke box bracket and must have been a strange sight when generating on a fairground."

THE ENGINES OF BILLY SMART

Billy Smart at Hayes End.

Known after the war years for his Circus fame, he was first a showman and these are Billy's engines, leading up to his circus days.

LITTLE MARGARET

Ealing 2/8/41. *Allan Downs collection.*

This is *Little Margaret* Fowler 14877, reg WY 3703, a 8 n.h.p. 2-speed 'Russian' type. It was new to the Ministry of Munitions in 1917. When the engine was only two years old it was sold to showman Willy Marshall of Bradford. He named it *Little Margaret* after his daughter. Mr Marshall fitted a crane to the engine and *Little Margaret* worked with his Chair-o-Planes.

In 1938 the new owner was Billy Smart who added a dynamo and new cab complete with brass uprights. In 1941, Billy put the engine on demolition work in the city. *Little Margaret* was first seen by Philip Bradley working on October 18th 1941.

This engine returned to the fairground in 1942, when the bulk of the demolition work had finished. It was photographed by Philip Bradley June 7th 1943 on Ealing Common, west London, winching up the centre truck of Billy's ride with Billy himself watching in the background.

Billy also bought another engine just for the London demolition work. Fowler 14902, reg FN 5031 originally belonged to Fred Gray around 1936. It was not named and now belonged to Billy Smart and was seen working on the London streets by Bradley on March 10th 1942.

NORAH

Almost at war, 1938. *Allan Downs collection.*

This is *Norah* a 7 n.h.p. Fowler 10302, reg KE 3895, built 1908, new to showman W. Arnold & Sons. In 1914 it was sold to showman John Botton & Sons, of Croydon. In 1934 a new firebox was fitted and a 200 amp dynamo. In 1939, it belonged to showman Billy Smart, who was very patriotic, as on the canopy was:

"CORONATION AMUSEMENTS – LONG LIVE THE KING"

and with crossed flags on the belly tank.

Bradley's first sighting of *Norah* working in London was October 4th 1941.

From the Peter Parrish collection.

In November 1941, a national newspaper mentioned this engine:

FROM FAIRGROUND TO BATTLEFIELD

This is 'Norah' she has not brought the swings and roundabouts. She has come along a unit among a fleet of tractors engaged in the sorry task of pulling the great walls that shook but did not fall when London was assaulted from the air. This is 'Norah' at work. It is a melancholy change from the cheerful noisy scenes of the fair ground, but she bears it bravely. All the brass rails and other bits of brass about her are shining bright and the painted inscriptions about the amusements, with which she is so honourable associated, remain, through somewhat dusty war work. 'Illuminator'another veteran of the fair ground and 'The Princess' are somewhere in the City.

After the war *Norah* did not return to the fairground and went to Hardwick's scrap yard in 1947.

THE PRINCESS

Photographer unknown. *From the Alan J. Martin collection.*

This one was also owned by Billy Smart. Fowler *The Princess* 14868, reg BN 5793 with "Long live the King" on her canopy. This was taken in Cannon Street, London, in 1941. St Paul's Cathedral can be seen in the background.

Road Loco Society collection.

The Princess was seen by Philip Bradley working on 4/10/41 and again 10/3/42.

THE EARLY YEARS

This engine was a 8 n.h.p. 2-speed, type R3 and was new to the Ministry of Munitions in 1917. It was then named *Little Lion.* It was designed for wood as her fuel and for service in Russia, but did not get that far, as you will see.

The next owner was showman Reuben Holdsworth of Bradford, Yorks. It travelled with his ride known as the Balloons & Flying Pigs. This was a steam-driven platform Round-a-bout with a huge wooden top.

By 1936 *Little Lion* was advertised in the 'World's Fair' by a Monty Goodman of Leeds. It came complete with dynamo and was £250. Billy Smart contacted Mr Goodman and consequently bought the engine. The first thing Billy did was spend money by adding twisted brass supports and lettering the canopy. By now her name had changed to *The Princess.*

Billy's Galloper centre and trucks. *The Bill Brian collection.*

Then in 1941, after five years generating and towing his rides, Billy put *The Princess* on demolition.

From the Bill Brian collection.

This one was the most photographed engine in London.

From the Hulton Archives. Copyright Fox/Getty.

It is thought she did return to showland again in 1942, after her work was done.

In 1947, Billy parted with his rides and concentrated more on his circus.

THE ENGINES OF FRED GRAY

DEMOLICIOUS

By Philip Bradley. Copyright the Surrey History Centre.

Look at the tyres – the rubble caused much damage to them and the wheels. Also this one has a belly tank in place of the original rope drum.

Demolicious was a Fowler class TE2 10 n.h.p. compound road locomotive, no 14916, reg no 1246, built in September 1917 and supplied to the Ministry of Munitions. At the end of the First World War she went to G E Millbank of Hatfield Heath, Essex. Then, in the early 1930s, was sold to showman Fred Gray of Hampstead Heath, who converted her into a showmen's engine. However, his son-in-law Charles Abbot, apart from driving her in the streets of London, must have had an ownership connection with the engine, as "Chas Abbott" was painted on the canopy. Originally this engine was named *Kathleen* and was re-named *Demolicious* in 1941. Charles Abbott named her whilst it was working on the demolition. Charles Abbotts son, said his father also had the engine christened properly by a vicar.

After the war it was sold to J. Biddall of Hounslow Middlesex. She never returned to showland duties, which is not surprising after what *Demolicious* went through. Eventually it was scrapped to J W Hardwick and Sons' well known yard at West Ewell.

Thank you to John Reeves for helping with this Information.

CONQUEROR

The Conqueror *1934.* *From the Road Loco Society collection.*

Burrell 3019, reg DP 4345, built in 1908 as a road engine for Charles Openshaw Ltd, Reading. The next to purchased her was G. Taylor of Redbourn, *The Conqueror* was not converted to a showmen's until 1931, when bought by London showman Fred Gray of Hampstead.

The photo was taken in 1934, by which time it had been converted to a showmen's, and had been in collision with a tramcar. Bradley also noted the number plate had changed to XH 8048, which is a registration on another of Gray's engines. After the accident, a new cab was fitted.

In 1941 Fred put this engine to demolition work. The wire rope on this one was 100 yards in length and it was seen January 9th 1941 by Philip Bradley working in the City. Fred must have put the registration right by this time, as he also had his other engine *Mons Star* also with reg XH 8048 working on the streets of London. *The Conqueror* was spotted again working on the demolition March 10th 1942 and was one of the few which did return to the fairgrounds, in 1943, now under the ownership of William Beach of Sunbury, Middlesex. It was scrapped c1949.

MONS STAR

Taken Mitcham Common, August 7th 1939.
By J. Wilkinson, from Allan Downs collection.

Burrell 2355 *Mons Star* XH 8048 was formerly owned by West Country showmen Hancocks and was known as *Lord Roberts.* After 18 years service it was sold to a former employee Fred Gray, who renamed it *Mons Star.* Along with several of his engines, Fred put *Mons Star* on demolition work in London.

It was spotted working by Philip Bradley October 4th 1941 in Mark Lane, London. This engine returned to the fairgrounds in May 1943 under the ownership of J Bond, then passed on to J. Biddall who retired her in 1947 and sent it to Hardwick's yard for scrap.

BLACK PRINCE

Burrell 2701 reg PE 7181.

From 1915 to 1935, this engine was well known around London for towing abnormal loads, while in the ownership of J.Hicky & Sons. In the early 20s it was one of the first to be fitted with the solid, endless, Mackintosh rubber traction tyres.

Eventually in the ownership of London showman Fred Gray, *Black Prince* was seen working in the city by Philip Bradley October 18th 1941, then he spotted it again six weeks later November 29 1941.

Black Prince was not seen again after this date working on the streets of London. However, this sad picture below was taken by Bradley, when he came across this engine again in 1942 at Hampstead. It shows 2701 covered over, yet demolition work was still being carried out in the streets.

By Philip Bradley. Copyright of the Surrey History Centre.

Was 2701 waiting for something? Bristol reporter 'The Bard' mentioned in his notes seeing 2701 under a different name and in Bristol.

WORLD'S FAIR 27/3/1943

By Bristol reporter 'The Bard'

Recently a showmen's type Burrell was engaged on demolition work in the city, and I noticed attracted a great deal of attention many times. I have seen it at work and always with a big crowd watching, but last week I notice a bigger crowd then usual.

Out of curiosity I mingled with the crowd. The attraction was a chalk-written message: "Driver wanted for this traction engine." I also noticed the contractor advertised in last week's 'World's Fair'.

WANTED
TRACTION ENGINE DRIVER FOR
DEMOLITION WORK AT BRISTOL
APPLY B&G TRANSPORT,
3 SOUTH COMMON,
REDBOURN, HERTS

The B&G transport, above, stood for two showmen's names, Biddle and Gray.

So, after the photo was taken by Philip Bradley, 2701, we believe, was transported to Bristol, as help was desperately needed. There had not been up to now, the engine power as in other cities for demolition.

Bristol had taken severe bombing as Hitler was targeting the Bristol Docks. 2701 is the only engine, so far, being reported working in two cities.

Road Loco Society collection.

With the war now over, this engine found its way to a scrap yard and spent some years rotting away. Because of the state of the canopy, I would say 2701 has been here a while but, there was light at the end of the tunnel, when she was rescued for preservation in 1962.

No 2701 **Black Prince,** ***restored.*** *Copyright of Barry J. Finch.*

I HAVE NO NAME AND WENT THROUGH HELL

Philip Bradley. Copyright of The Surrey History Centre.

Un-named was a 3-speed, 6 n.h.p. Fowler 12435, reg AD 8804. New May 30th 1912 for Barmby Bendalls Furniture Removals of Cheltenham. After two more owners, one of which only paid £35 at auction, it then went to Fred Gray of Hampstead in about 1934.

It travelled with Gray's Gallopers until 1937, then ride and engine were laid up in the yard for a time. That is where the engine photo was taken.

Later, the gallopers were out again; the photo below was taken on the Hampstead Vale of Health for the 'Holiday at Home' fair.

From the Bill Brian collection.

In 1941, Fred put the engine on the London demolition. This particular engine Philip Bradley reported seeing with its cab smashed up from falling masonry. Then in the blitz of October 5th 1941, due to being hit by an incendiary bomb, the engine caught fire, relieving it of its partial canopy, all the rubber on the wheels and, of course, anything combustible. Apart from that, the engine was fine, just completely blackened but it was still able to work!

A year later Bradley reported it being still without a canopy and:

"A strange sight with its cab support rods still sticking up into thin air".

I think we can presume this one must have ended up at Hardwick's, like so many of the others.

Photo By Barry J. Finch.

This is not the engine in our story, however this was the ending for many, at Hardwick's the engine graveyard.

OLYMPIC

Foster 12468 reg XC 9637 at Hampstead.
By Philip Bradley. Copyright of Surrey History Centre.

The following was written by fairground enthusiast Philip Bradley:

"In one small area of the city, where innumerable tall buildings were damaged beyond repair, it seemed uncanny about the sight of in the midst of such devastation, a greater number of showmen's engines, that had been congregated on any one fairground for a long time. I clearly remember seeing the Foster 'Olympic,' absolutely smothered in masonry dust, proceeding at a good speed up the Pentonville Road in the direction of Hampstead. I managed to reach Hampstead first. On its arrival the belt was immediately fitted, and it was running Mrs Gray's Chair-o-Planes within minutes."

Olympic was seen again by Bradley on October 18th 1941.

Allan Downs collection.

So *Olympic* was a pulling down buildings by day then rushing back to power the ride at night. The above can help us appreciate how hard these engines can work. In 1942, when the demolition work was over, and she was still under Fred Gray's ownership, *Olympic* continued on the fairgrounds.

In the late spring of 1942 the most dangerous buildings in and around London had been demolished and now it was just a small amount of clearing up that needed doing. The bombing had petered out in 1942, due to Hitler putting his resources into attacking Russia. On March 10th there were still 12 engines working in London, but by late June only 4 engines were there, *Olympic* Foster 12468 being one of them.

HARRY GRAY

Between 1919 and 1921 Frederick Gray ordered two new Burrell special scenic showmen's road locomotives. One of the engines, no. 3884 *Wonder*, was delivered on 14/3/21 and no. 3886 *Lord Lascelle's* one month later on 13/4/21. Both were ordered to Burrell's full 'special scenic' specification.

Soon after Fred had taken delivery of 3886 *Lord Lascelles* it is understood his son, Harry, asked if he could use the engine. So, *Wonder* (later re-named *Gladiator*) 3884 remained with Fred and 3886 *Lord Lascelles* with Harry. Evidence confirms that 3886 was taken over by Harry Gray soon after its delivery but was still occasionally used by Fred.

During its working life, 3886 was frequently seen hauling and powering Harry Gray's rides, including his four-abreast gallopers, Coronation Ark, Dodgems, Swirl, Steam Yachts and other rides over its 18-year operational life.

D. Hayward.

Harry used *Lord Lascelles* on the fairground until the end of the 1939 season, by which time Britain was at war. Then the engine was parked in Harry's yard at Mitcham, Surrey.

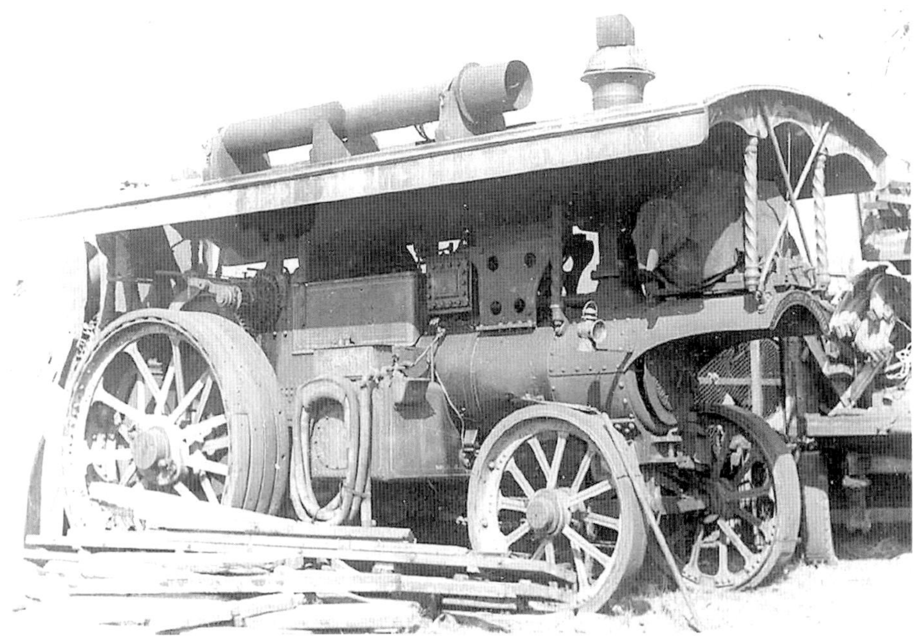

By Philip Bradley. Copyright of Surrey History Centre.

In 1941 Harry, like his father, could see money could be made with the engine which was now standing idle. London showman Charles Abbot said he and his father not only drove engine *Demolicious* but were also drivers on *Lord Lascelles*, so we know Harry put 3886 to demolition work on the streets of London. This would have been only for a **short time**, after which it returned to the yard until 1951 when it was sent to Hardwicks scrap yard. However, the engine was not scrapped but the name was changed to *Tulyar* after that year's Epsom Derby winner. Also Hardwicks had their name painted on the canopy side panels. It was only in their ownership for a year then in 1952 the boilermakers James Hickey & Sons of Cheshunt, Herts. bought the engine for preservation.

Lord Lascelles was fully dismantled when, sadly, Mr Hickey died in 1954 before the rebuilding work was completed. The engine then passed to his eldest son but no more work was carried out and it remained in pieces until young Mr Hickey died in 1964 aged only 44.

Steve Neville of Saffron Walden, Essex, a senior employee at Hickey's, was appointed by the family to oversee the closure of the business. He bought *Lord Lascelles* in pieces from the Hickey estate, owning her from 1964-1980 during which time he restored the engine to her original showland glory and rallied her extensively.

Although Harry Gray had removed *Lord Lascelles'* dynamo in 1939 it remained traceable from its brass plate bearing his name and indeed many years later it was brought back and refitted to the engine. In 1995, Lord Lascelles, the man himself, stood on the foot plate of the engine.

Thank you to Mr Richard Marsh for this information.

We finish here with the engines on the London demolition and with a unique photo, which was found by chance in a Dutch archive. It shows Harry Grays fair, open in London in 1947. The engines have long gone by now, but this is unique, as it is a photo of a fairground through a charred window of a bombed building left behind by the showmen's engines.

MELTDOWN

Due to the demand for munitions many engines went for scrap. You could not fail to notice how Hardwicks scrap dealers took in many engines, as their name appears a number of times in this book.

Photo from Mr Ron Dawe.

This is not one of our engines, as this is Burrell no 3804 *Independence,* but this was the outcome for most of our engines.

In 1942, the demolition was coming to an end for our engines, however the demand for metal was ongoing.

This showman appeared in a 1944 addition of the 'World's Fair':

£525 DAMAGES FOR SHOWMAN

At Leeds Assizes, Mr Enoch Farrar, a Rotherham showman, was awarded £525 + costs, from J.W. Eyre & Co Ltd scrap metal merchants of Sheffield. At the hearing it was stated Mr Farrar bought a 6 hp Scenic type road loco in 1938, he paid £2,012 for the engine to drive the lights on the Yorkshire Scenic Railway, also the engine had been seen in the past driving the organ and lights at a recital.

Now Mr Farrar had it laid up on a farm at Maltby, nr Rotherham. Mr Farrar went to see the engine as he periodically did and in April 1941, he went to see the engine and it had vanished. Mr Farrar had no knowledge of the affair and enquiries had to be made. It was discovered Eyre & Co had purchased the engine from a man who now had since passed away, the engine was then cut for scrap.

We have also mentioned some of the rides these engines worked with, however, rides as well as engines were being sent to the melting pot. This article appeared in a 1942 'World's Fair' paper:

TANKS FROM DODGEMS

Dodgem cars, Ghost Trains, Scenic Railways and Round-a-Bouts are going to make tanks, bombs and guns. Several hundred tons from famous amusement parks in sea side towns, have been presented to the Ministry of Works by Butlins Ltd. The task of sorting and removal has been put to hand.

DISMANTLING OF RIDES

Disused riding machines that belong to Welsh showman Mr Studt, have now been dismantled at Clydach fair ground and the materials handed over for National purposes.

This showman really did want to help and this is his letter to the 'World's Fair':

> *Sir*
>
> *may I make an appeal to fellow showmen of Great Britain, who have any unused Round-a-bouts, swings, ENGINES, dynamos, etc. To collect same and let the country have them for munitions. Collect from your wagon Back boxes, Belly Boxes any stakes, old nuts, bolts, screws, old tools and paraffin lamps, trace chains and all the old junk. Let the Government have it to master those inhuman brutes who are killing and wounding children whose happy little faces and pennies have kept our wheels turning, and who will never see again all the fun of the fair.*
>
> *Yours etc*
> *Ex Gunner PAT COLLINS*

TARGETED

The scrap dealers would make a beeline for showmen's yards as they were known for their metal parts lying around, i.e. parts of riding machines, lorries and of course the occasional traction engine. Messrs Herberts of Dorchester, Dorset owned *Houpla*, Burrell no 3063, reg CR 5893. Jack Herbert bought her from new and had many years use from the engine, including towing for the military during WWI. Just before WWII, the boiler failed.

Soon after war was declared two scrap dealers walked into Jack's yard and asked "*Got any old bits about you don't want Mr Herbert*?" *Houpla* was parked up in the corner and all of a sudden became centre of attention. She weighed 12 tons and scrap was £1 per ton at the time, so Jack had £12 plus a little extra for the brass.

Information and photo supplied by Mr Eddie Herbert.

We can only wonder now, if Hitler had not shown his ugly hand, how many of those engines we lost would have made it into preservation. We are also now left with the sad thought of how those engines that were cut up and melted down for ammunition, ended up being fragments of shrapnel scattered over Europe. Or should we look at it from another point of view, that the showmen's engines played an important part in preserving our freedom?

FROM STEAM TO LORRY

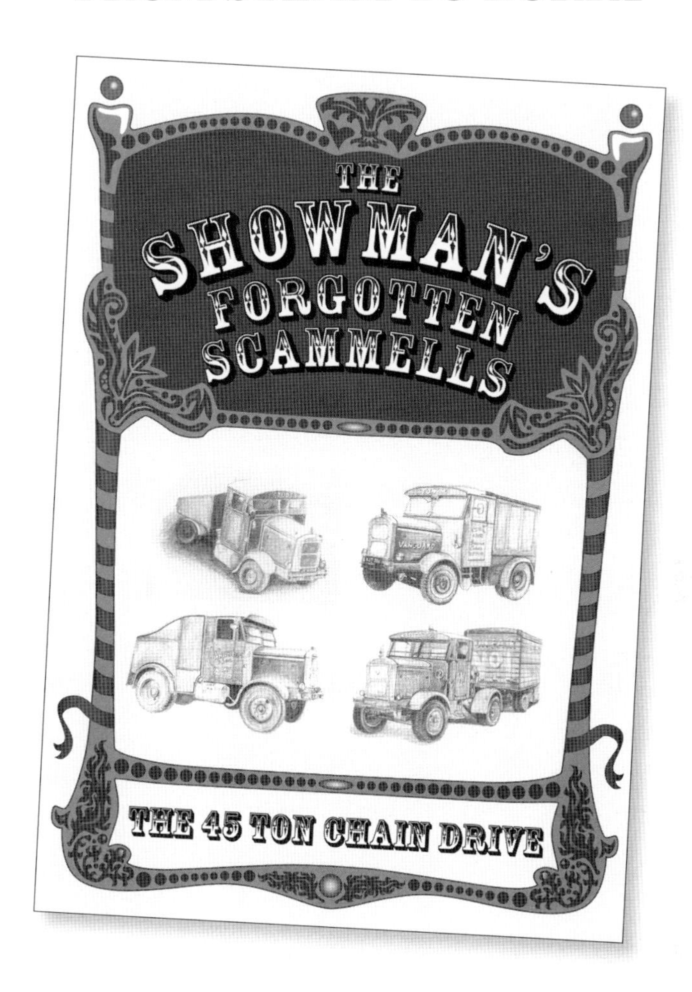

In 1946, the last 10 new 45 ton chain drive Scammells at Watford went to the showmen. Some carried the name of former traction engines and also took on the roll of towing and powering the rides. This book tells of the life of each Scammell on the road.

For your copy
please send £13.95 to:

K Townsend
9, Putton Lane
Charlestown
Weymouth
Dorset
DT3 4AE

My next book, now in preparation, will be of the fairgrounds during WWII. How the showmen bought their own Spitfire and with tales from showmen who served their country.

THE BOOK CHARTS THE LIFE OF THE SHOWMEN AND WHAT THEY SUFFERED, INCLUDING:

1939 most fairs cancelled, with many showmen driven from the business

Police search living wagons and confiscate radios

Show families must have correct ration books, or no food

Rifle-range bore shortage, so restricted opening for shooters

Propaganda printed against showmen

Few drivers, their men drained away by the Services,

Stall prize shortage

To stay open, so to keep up civilian morale

Incendiary bombs burn rides

Living wagons peppered with bullets

Doodlebug heading for the ride

Living wagons destroyed

Penny Arcade blown to pieces

And still they kept going. How did they survive this? With information never been printed before, this book will even tell the young showmen of today what they never knew about the past. Transport will be included.